Cromosys Publication

Teach Yourself Spanish

NIRANJAN JHA SHOWMAN

Founder - Niranjan Jha Showman
cromosys®
Corporation
Education and Technology Research Center
Patankar Park, Nallasopara (W), Mumbai. +91-9561450045
Education, Technology, Publication, Healthcare, Newsmedia, Realtor, Filmmaking
www.facebook.com/cromosys

+91-9561450045
Learn Advanced Skills
And Get Job Instantly
GERMAN
Python
FRENCH
C++
SPANISH
Java
ENGLISH
HTML5
RUSSIAN
CSS
JavaScript
Cromosys
Education and Technology Research Center
Nallasopara (W), Mumbai

Learn Web Programming
Demo-Class Free
HTML
CSS
React
JavaScript
Typescript
Bootstrap
Cromosys
20 Years of Experience
Nallasopara (W), Mumbai
+91-9561450045

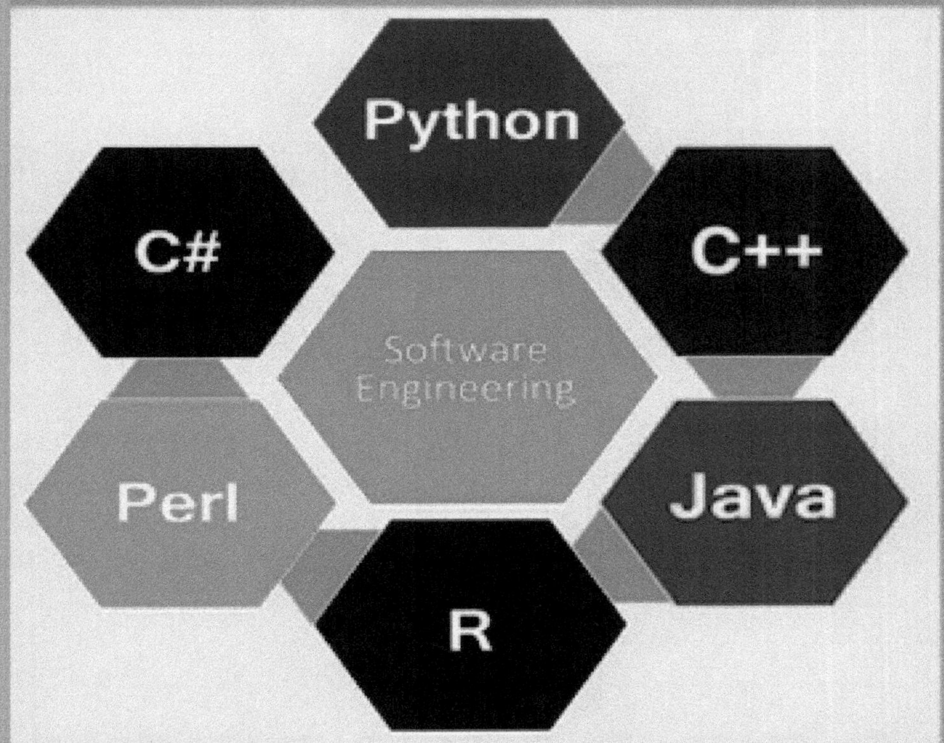

+91-9561450045
Learn Software Engineering
Demo-Class Free
Python
C#
C++
Software
Engineering
Perl
Java
R
Cromosys
20 Years of Experience
Nallasopara (W), Mumbai
+91-9561450045

25 Years of Experience
Learn Visual Multimedia

Animation VFX
Movie Editing
Game Development

Cromosys
+91-9561450045
Education and Technology Research Center
Nallasopara (W), Mumbai
www.facebook.com/cromosys

Jobs Available
For Candidates Who Know

German

French

Spanish

Vacancy in Germany, France, Spain

For Hospitality, Engineering, IT Sector

With Free Visa, Airfare and Accommodation

Cromosys
Education and Technology Research Centre
Nallasopara (W), Mumbai
+91-9561450045
20 Years of Experience

+91-9561450045
Foreign Languages Institute
German, French, Spanish
Basic and Advanced - All Levels
3 x 6 = 18 Courses
FRANCHISE
Business Offer
Teaching Materials Provided
We have 1 Million Students Globally
Great Income Assured
Global Exposure
Cromosys
20 Years of Experience
Nallasopara (W), Mumbai
+91-9561450045

Cromosys Publication

Teach Yourself Spanish

Niranjan Jha Showman

"Education taken with zeal educes to success."
~Niranjan Showman

Preface

Cromosys Publication's "Teach Yourself Spanish" book is an optimal quality guide to the beginners as well as advanced learners. Spanish is the language of great demand after English as it is widely spoken in many European countries. Language is the pillar of human origin and evolution, and so, even many other languages of the world died in this century, but Spanish is still surviving and flourishing because of its strong root in human culture and civilization. Moreover, the grammar of Spanish language is the base of English grammar too. This book is unmatchable and unique of its kind that guarantees your success. The lessons and study materials exclusively designed are based on my fifteen years of research in linguistic field. The text, audio and video are magnificently powerful to bring you into educational light. Whether your intention is to work, travel abroad or plunge deep into your research, if you need to learn a language, then Spanish is the best choice.

Around eight years ago, when I went to the USA, I got a chance to learn it, and since then I have been teaching this language globally with high exposure. Having been communicating with Spanish-speaking people around the world while managing a team in several call centers, and being able to understand linguistic science, I would like to assure you that this language is easy to learn in just one moth of daily practice. And once learnt, with your sharpened bilingual ability, you can make your way of success without any hindrance. After you start the lesson of this book, you don't need to worry about anything but just follow each and every lesson carefully. Don't procrastinate and never give up. You are going to do the most beautiful thing for yourself, so be bold enough to complete all the lessons. The sentence constructions of Spanish are similar to English, only a few things which are not similar, I have explained properly in the easiest method I could ever find. The pronunciation of each word is given in bracket to help you speak correctly.

The significance of this book is that it is dynamic, systemic and blissful with abundance of pure and perfect set of rules that took a decade of time in preparation. One being immaturely suggested, spends ages in watching movies and listening to the audio in lure of learning Spanish. But it doesn't bring success as they imitate a little but don't learn what in actual sense Spanish is. And their never-ending process of Picasso Adventure collects some scattered information which is unworthy to learning a foreign language. So the aspirants get lost in wilderness. You may have seen some other books on Spanish full of conversations and dialogues which the students purchase by mistake, but they quit learning soon because those are not the proper books. Just memorizing the dialogues will not take you anywhere. So I have designed this book with proper set of lessons to make you start your adventure sitting at home beginning with real basic. This book is highly useful for people working in communication based industry, media houses, entertainment world, and for those who are teachers, writers, researchers and students. And definitely for those who love languages – especially Spanish!

Cromosys, our education and technology research center, saving human efforts from being wasted, is dedicated to teach you this language as good as possible. The world growing with density has brought enormous opportunity to foreign language speakers irrespective of their geographical boundaries. Having been teaching this language from several years, I have come across numerous unique rules which I have elaborated and explained in this book. Our path-breaking pioneer training institute, Cromosys, is committed to enlightening human mind with educational endeavors, and we are doing the same from fifteen successful years. I believe I have done all that I could to make this book useful to you, and not only hopeful but I am sure that your success is in your hand now because this book will take you miles ahead in your expectation. We always respect the views and comments of readers, so for any communication with regards to assistance, enquiry or collaboration, we are always at your reach as it helps us improve our ability.

Niranjan Jha Showman
Trainer, Author, Physician, Entrepreneur, Filmmaker, Activist
Founder of Cromosys Corporation
facebook.com/cromosys
+91-9561450045
cromosys@yahoo.com
Nallasopara (W), Mumbai, India

My other books: -
English Voice Accent and Pronunciation
Teach Yourself German
Teach Yourself French
Teach Yourself Spanish
Be millionaire like me
Dynamic Grammar of English
Teach Yourself HTML5
Teach Yourself 3ds Max
Teach Yourself Autodesk Maya

Cromosys Corporation
Education and Technology Research Center
Education, Technology, Publication, Healthcare, Realtor, Filmmaking
facebook.com/cromosys
+91-9561450045
cromosys@yahoo.com
Nallasopara (W), Mumbai, India

About the Author

Niranjan Jha Showman
Trainer, Author, Physician, Entrepreneur, Filmmaker, Activist

Niranjan Jha Showman is a Language Scientist and Technical Researcher. He is the Award Winning author of more than fifty educational and fictional books at Amazon. He is one of the great-grandsons of the first President of India Dr. Rajendra Prasad. He is a Public Figure, and the globally - renowned Languages Trainer of French, Spanish, and German from past twenty years. Niranjan Jha Showman is an Entrepreneur and also works as a Filmmaker in India. Being the founder and owner of Cromosys Corporation - a company located in Mumbai, India, his company is excelling in the fields of Education, Technology, Publication, Newsmedia, Realtors, Banking, and Cinemascope from past fifteen years.

Niranjan Jha Showman's good-seller educational books and novels are appreciated worldwide. He has more than one million eBook buyers online, and more than one million learners are connected to him globally. One of his novels is critically acclaimed. He is the trainer of French, Spanish, German, English Voice and Accent, and Advanced Computer Education. He is also a political activist in India.

Niranjan Jha Showman is the man who came from rags to riches, he who knows how to turn the table, and he, whom you call the man of Midas-touch. He has observed lives from the Pandora of monkeys to the sanctuary of monks, not only down-to-earth but down-to-grave. He is a B. Com. graduate, and B. Ed. from Delhi University, and diploma holder in French, Spanish and German from America. You can watch his songs, movies, educational videos and many more things by typing "Niranjan Jha Showman" in Google.

Niranjan Jha Showman
+91-9561450045
cromosys@yahoo.com
Mumbai, India
facebook.com/cromosys

Statutory

This book with its content is the registered property of the author Niranjan Jha Showman.
The author and his Cromosys Publication holds all necessary rights of this book.
The copyright certificate of this book is attached at the end of this book.

Lesson 1

Alphabet

There are 29 letters in Spanish alphabet. Next to each letter, its name as pronunciation is given. Write the letter in your notebook and speak out the pronunciation of it for practice. Please don't jump up to the next lesson without proper practice of this lesson.

A	aa	
B	be	(as 'bay')
C	the	('th' as 'thin' in English)
CH	che	(as 'chay')
D	de	(as 'day')
E	e	(as 'ay')
F	effe	
G	khe	(heavy 'kh')
H	aache	
I	ee	
J	khotaa	
K	kaa	
L	elle	
LL	ellye	
M	emme	
N	enne	
Ñ	ennye	
O	o	
P	pe	(as 'pay')
Q	koo	
R	erre	
S	esse	(as 'essay')
T	te	(as 'tay')
U	oo	
V	oobhe	
W	ubhe dobhle	
X	ekees	
Y	eegregaa	
Z	thetaa	('th' as 'thin' in English)

The letter 'CH' and 'LL' are officially removed from Spanish in 2010.
The letter V is pronounced 'oobhe' as 'b' and 'v' are pronounced same.
The letter V generally sounds 'b' or 'bh' in Spanish language.
Z is pronounced 'thetaa' in original Spanish, but 'setaa' in Latin America.

Lesson 2

Pronunciation of Vowels

The Spanish vowels are a, e, i, o and u. Each vowel has only one sound when used in a word. The Spanish vowel sounds are similar to English.

a is pronounced 'aa'
For example:

Spanish Word	Pronunciation	Meaning
al	(aal)	to
la	(laa)	the
casa	(kaasaa)	house

e is pronounced 'e'

Spanish Word	Pronunciation	Meaning
me	(me) as 'may'	me
de	(de) as 'day'	from
le	(le) as 'lay'	him

i is pronounced big 'ee' not small 'i'

Spanish Word	Pronunciation	Meaning
mi	(mee)	my
prima	(preema)	first

o is pronounced 'o'

Spanish Word	Pronunciation	Meaning
no	(no)	no
gato	(gaato)	cat

u is pronounced 'oo'

Spanish Word	Pronunciation	Meaning
tu	(too)	your
su	(soo)	their
uno	(oono)	one

A is pronounced 'aa', but native speaker may pronounce it 'ae' – as 'c**a**t' in English.
Original Spanish is called Castilian Spanish as Castile region in Spain gave birth to Spanish.
Words with multiple meanings are explained later in this book.

Lesson 3

Pronunciation of Consonants

There only two consonants **z** and **j** which are pronounced differently from English. Other consonants are pronounced almost same as in English.

z is pronounced 'th' as in English 'mouth' or 'thick'.

luz	(looth)	light
voz	(bhoth)	voice
zapato	(thapaato)	shoe

j is pronounced differently in Spanish. '**j**' sounds like heavy guttural sound of '**kh'**coming from inner part of throat as 'ch' sound of the word 'auch' in German, or 'ch' sound of 'loch' in Scottish and 'kh' of 'Khan' in Arabic. It is an aspirated sound with 'h' coming from inner throat which does not exist in English.

caja	(kaakhaa)	box
lejos	(lekhos)	far
jugar	(khoogar)	to play
ojo	(okho)	eye

ñ is pronounced like 'ny' as 'companion' in English. (n+y)

niño	(neenyo)	child
señor	(senyor)	mister
mañana	(maanyana)	tomorrow, morning

c before e or i is pronounced like 'th' otherwise it is pronounced 'k'.

cena	(thenaa)	dinner
once	(onthe)	eleven
caro	(kaaro)	expensive

g before e or i is pronounced like heavy 'kh' otherwise it is pronounced 'g' as in English 'go'.

coger	(kokher)	to catch
gente	(khente)	people
lugar	(loogaar)	place

Z is pronounced 'th' in European Spanish, but 's' in Latin America.
The word 'voz' is pronounced – (bhoth), (both), (bos).

h is not pronounced at all.

hasta	(aastaa)	until
hacia	(aathyaa)	towards
hola	(olaa)	hello
hijo	(eekho)	son

ch, **qu**, **gu** are pronounced same as in English.

r is rolled on the tip of tongue more than English.

gorra	(goraa)	cap
barrio	(baaryo)	district
rosa	(rosaa)	rose

s is always pronounced 's' as in English 'see' or 'same' , not like 'z' in 'easy'.

camisa	(kameesa)	shirt
sol	(sol)	sun
bolso	(bolso)	bag

y is like 'y' as in 'yes' – but 'y' at the end of a word is pronounced like 'i'

yo	(yo)	I
playa	(plaayaa)	beach
soy	(soi)	I am

Special note:-

s is always like 'ss' as in 'missing' , never like 's' in 'easy'.
a always sounds like 'aa' as in 'harm' or 'cast' never like 'a' in 'hat'.
The letter '**o**' in Spanish is pronounced 'o' as in 'not'.
th should always be pronounced 'th' as in 'thin' , not like 'th' in 'they'.
ll coming together in a word is pronounced 'y' , not 'l'.
You need to be careful at '**j**' as it pronounced 'kh' not 'j',
When '**l**' comes alone in a word (not 'll'), then it sounds 'l'.
The word 'morning' can be referred by two words: matutino, mañana.

Spanish has a lot of complex situations that are be explained later in this book.

Lesson 4

The Accent
Spanish has three types of accent which are placed as stroke on certain letters as explained below. Having proper knowledge of this lesson helps you write Spanish words with correct spelling.

1. Acute Accent: The Acute Accent comes on vowel – a, e, i, o, u. This accent (') is used on some words to distinguish words which have the same spelling but different meanings. All pair words have same pronunciation, and this pair is for only some words. The other two accents are explained at the bottom.

el the
él he
si if
sí yes
mi my
mí me
mas but
más more

Punctuation Marks

Question marks and exclamation marks are placed at both end of a sentence and the first one is placed inverted like upside-down.

¿Cómo? (komo) How?
¿Por qué? (por ke) Why?
¿Dónde? (donde) Where?
¿Cuándo? (kwaando) When?
¿Quién? (kyen) Who/Whom?
¿Qué? (ke) What?
¿Cuál? (kwaal) Which/What?
¿De quién? (de kyen) Whose?

2. The second accent, **diaresis (¨)** is placed over u to pronounce (ü) separately if it comes after 'g'. The letter 'ü' sounds as minor (u) of English.

agüero (aagu-ero) omen

3. The third accent, **tilde (˜)** is placed over n, when 'n' is to be pronounced like 'ny' in 'onion'.

mañana (maanyaana) morning

The letter 'qu' is always pronounced 'k'.
Qué means 'what' but Que means 'that'.

Strict Instructions

Remember that learning Spanish is never difficult. The only thing you have to do is that take this book as a guide to lead you step by step. Till now, you have completed five lessons. Up to here, things were easy, but now it will get complex as you move ahead. For that, it requires proper practice by writing the lesson from this book into your notebook and practicing the pronunciation of the words. If you ignore and do not do this, lessons from here will look difficult to you. So before moving ahead, make sure you have done proper practice till fifth lesson.

Just looking into this book with pleasure seeking attitude can make you laugh a little, as you see some words of Spanish, but if you are really interested to learn, then be serious about it. Don't jump off and scroll down to the other pages without having proper practice done on all the previous lessons. Why it is necessary is that while learning a foreign language, even your single mistake will push your so much down, from where you can't even think of starting back again. If English is your first language, imagine how the other people learn it! I can tell you, English is also not easy to billions of people of the world. Many learn English after great efforts.

In the same way, you have to make efforts to learn this language. You won't learn it automatically, because if it was so easy, there was no need to buy this book. You would have learnt it by yourself. There are many people who want to learn a new language because it is very much fascinating, but many of them fail in the beginning only because they don't practice. For them, grapes are sour!

What is easy in the world? And if something is easy, what benefit the easy thing can give you? Nothing. If you want great success, you have to do great work. Remember that only difficult thing brings amazing success in your life. So refrain yourself from behaving like a play-boy learner and be a little serious about it – about Spanish.

(1) You can enjoy the world of Spanish only after you completely go through this book.
(2) Once you are thorough, you may need to buy a Spanish-to-English dictionary.
(3) After this book, you may refer to my next book: Foreign Languages Conversation.
(4) Google Translate will help you a lot in learning while going through this book.
(5) If you get a chance to communicate with native Spanish, it will be fabulous.

Wishing you all the best! Don't quit, continue learning.

Capital and Small Letters:-

A sentence begins with a capital letter.
Proper nouns begin with a capital letter.
The name of a country begins with a capital letter.
But the inhabitants begin with small letter.

The letter 'd' is pronounced as – soft d, and letter 't' as – soft t.
Words with accent marks are adopted from Latin having very soft usage.

Lesson 5

Nouns and Gender
In Spanish, all nouns are either masculine or feminine. There are no neuter nouns. Most of the nouns ending with the letter **o** are masculine. Most of the nouns ending with **a, ión, d, z** are feminine. However, there are some exceptions.

Masculine nouns

el guardia	(gwaardyaa)	the policeman
el lápiz	(laapeeth)	the pencil
el camión	(kaamyon)	the lorry
el idioma	(eedyoma)	the language
el mapa	(maapaa)	the map
el hombre	(ombre)	the man
el mar	(maar)	the sea
el caballo	(kaabaayo)	the horse
el éxito	(ekseeto)	the success
el premio	(premyo)	the prize

*el = the (used for masculine noun)

Feminine nouns

la mujer	(mookher)	the woman
la mano	(maano)	the hand
la galleta	(gaayetaa)	the biscuit
la ropa	(ropaa)	the clothes
la hermana	(ermaanaa)	the sister
la manzana	(maanthaanaa)	the apple
la cocina	(kotheenaa)	the kitchen
la maleta	(maaletaa)	the suitcase
la taza	(taathaa)	the cup
la pelota	(pelotaa)	the ball

*la = the (used for feminine noun)

Exercise:-
Write English meaning of these words in your notebook.
la taza, el mar, el hombre,casa, caro, zapato, mañana, prima, la cocina, la mano, el camión, el éxito, la hermana, el guardia, la pelota, la maleta, el mapa

Write Spanish meaning of these words in your notebook.
the map, where, when, how, morning, yes, if, but, more, shirt, sun, bag, I, son, place, dinner, child, tomorrow, the man, the sea, the horse, the success, the woman, the hand, the biscuit

The letter 'h' is kept silent when it comes in the beginning of a word.
There is no fixed rule to recognize gender of nouns.

Lesson 6

Singular – Plural Nouns

The plural of nouns is formed by adding '**s**' to the nouns ending with a vowel.

hombre	(ombre)	man
hombres	(ombres)	men
libro	(leebro)	book
libros	(leebros)	books
casa	(kaasaa)	house
casas	(kaasaas)	houses

The plural of nouns is formed by adding '**es**' to the nouns ending with a consonant.

mujer	(mookher)	woman
mujeres	(mookheres)	women
ciudad	(thyoodaad)	town
ciudades	(thyoodaades)	towns
hostal	(ostaal)	hotel
hostales	(ostaales)	hotels

The plural of nouns ending with **z** is formed by changing the **z** into **c** and adding **es**.

lápiz	(laapeeth)	pencil
lápices	(laapeethes)	pencils
luz	(looth)	light
luces	(loathes)	lights

Nouns ending with a consonant and bearing an accent on the last syllable (part of the word) of a word loses that accent while forming plural.

camión	(kaamyon)	lorry
camiónes	(kaamyones)	lorries
jardín	(khaardeen)	garden
jardines	(khaardeenes)	gardens

Exercise:-
Change these nouns into plural forms.

lápiz, jardín, mujer, libro, hombre, camión, casa, mano, hermana, pelota, idioma, caballo, premio, maleta, hostal, manzana

Lesson 7

Articles

Articles (a or the) agree with gender and number of the noun. If the noun is masculine and singular, then the article being used with it should also be masculine singular only. If the noun is feminine singular, then the article would also be feminine singular only.

The use of indefinite article 'a' , 'some'.

Article		Use with word	Meaning
un	(masculine singular)	un libro	a book
una	(feminine singular)	una casa	a house
unos	(masculine plural)	unos libros	some books
unas	(feminine plural)	unas casas	some houses

The use of definite article 'the'.

Article		Use with word	Meaning
el	(masculine singular)	el libro	the book
la	(feminine singular)	la casa	the house
los	(masculine plural)	los libros	the books
las	(feminine plural)	las casas	the houses

There is no 'an' article, but masculine article 'un' or 'el' is used before a feminine singular noun word which begins with the letter **a** or **ha**. It happens to establish proper pronunciation.

el agua   the water
el hambre   the hunger

(agua and hambre are feminine singular nouns. Instead of article 'la' **el** is used in the example).

Exercise:-
Write the meaning of these words in English.
los libros, el hambre, las casas, el agua, las mujeres, un hombre, la mujer, la cocina, la mano, el camión, el éxito, la hermana, el guardia, la pelota, la maleta, una casa, un libro

Write the meaning of these words in Spanish.
a policeman, some policemen, the policeman, the policemen, a woman, some women, the woman, the women, the house, the water, a man, the man

Lesson 8

Singular Pronouns

yo	I	
tú	thou	(familiar form)
él	he	
ella	she	
usted	you	(polite form)

Plural Pronouns

nosotros	we	(masculine)
nosotras	we	(feminine)
vosotros	thou people	(masculine familiar form)
vosotras	thou people	(feminine familiar form)
ellos	they	(masculine)
ellas	they	(feminine)
ustedes	you people	(polite form)

The familiar form is used with the person who is familiar and friendly to you. **tú** can be used for the member of the family, friends, children and animals.

The polite forms **usted** and **ustedes** are the most useful pronouns used to address all other people. In writing, instead of **usted** and **ustedes**, **Vd.** and **Vds.** are used which is the full-form of **Vuestra Merced** means 'your mercy.

Further you will find that except **usted** and **ustedes**, other pronouns are generally used very less in Spanish. This is the peculiarity of Spanish.

Exercise:-
Write the meaning of these words in English.
ella, nosotros, tú, él, ellos, vosotras, ustedes, nosotras, yo

Lesson 9

Forms of address

There are three titles used to address someone:

Titles	Short forms	Meaning
señor	Sr.	Mr.
señora	Sra.	Mrs.
señorita	Srta.	Miss

While writing, to address someone first you have to use the definite articles 'el' or 'la' , then this title, and then the person's name. But, at the time of direct talking you do not have to use 'el' or 'la'.

El Sr. Martínez.	Mr. Martinez.
La Sra. Martínez.	Mrs. Martinez.
La Srta. Martínez.	Miss Martinez.
Por aqí, Sr. Martínez.	This way, Mr. Martinez.

The title **Don** and **Doña** is used in front of a person's Christian name:

Don Juan (pronounced – khuaan)
Doña Maria

Exercise:-
Translate them into Spanish.
Miss Carmen, Mr. Jackson, Mrs. Fernandez, Miss Peterson, Mrs. Sutherland, Mr. Abraham, Miss Clark, Mr. Bradley

Lesson 10

Contraction of article

Preposition **'a'** means **to** (pronounced – 'aa')

a jardín   to garden
a casa   to house
a mujer   to woman

Preposition **'de'** means **of** or **from** (pronounced – soft 'de')

de jardín   of/from garden
de casa   of/from house
de mujer   of/from woman

But, when preposition 'a' contracts with article 'el' or 'la' , it becomes **'al'** (pronounced – 'aal')

al jardín   to the garden
al casa   to the house
al mujer   to the woman

When preposition 'de' contracts with article 'el', it becomes **'del'**. But no change with 'la'.

del jardín   of/from the garden (masculine)
de la casa   of/from the house (feminine)
de la mujer   of/from the woman (feminine)

And the possession must be expressed using 'de' preposition like this:

El padre de Juan.   The father of John / John's father
El paraguas del niño.   The umbrella of the child / The child's umbrella

But this contraction is not applicable with indefinite article 'a'.
To a garden   a un jardein

Exercise:-
Translate them into Spanish.
to the town, of the town, to the hotel, of the hotel, to the man, of the man, to the woman, to the house,
to the garden, from the garden, from the house, from the woman, to the child, of the child

New words: padre – father, paraguas – umbrella

Lesson 11

The Adjectives

Adjectives agree in gender and number with the nouns they qualify. The adjectives which end with the letter **'o'** agreeing with masculine noun, the **'o'** changes to **'a'** when it agrees with a feminine noun. The plural of the adjective is formed by adding **'s'** to the both gender.

El coche blanco.   The white car.
La casa blanca.   The white house.
Los coches blancos.   The white cars.
Las casas blancas.   The white houses.

Most of the adjectives ending with a consonant or the letter **'e'** have the same form for masculine and feminine. The plural is formed by adding **'s'** to those ending with **'e'** and **'es'** to those ending with a consonant.

Un ejercicio fácil.   An easy exercise.   (ekhertheethyo fatheel)
Una lección fácil.   An easy lesson.   (lekthyon)
Unos ejercicios fáciles.   Some easy exercises.   (ekhertheethyos fatheeles)
Unas lecciones fáciles.   Some easy lessons.

El lápiz verde.   The green pencil.
La pared verde.   The green wall.
Los lápices verdes.   The green pencils.
Las paredes verdes.   The green walls.

Exceptions to this rule are:

español   Spanish (m)
española   Spanish (f)
inglés   English (m)
inglesa   English (f)
trabajador   hardworking (m)
trabajadora   hardworking (f)
holgazán   lazy (m)
holgazana   lazy (f)

Exercise:-Translate them into Spanish.
the red car, the red cars, the blue house, the blue houses, the white wall, the white walls, the blue pencil, the blue pencils

New words: coche – car, blanco – white, ejercicio – exercise, fácil – easy, lección – lesson, lápiz – pencil, verde – green, red – rojo, blue – azul

As you noticed, adjectives are used after noun.

Lesson 12

Demonstrative Adjectives

Demonstrative adjective is always used before noun and agree with it in gender and number.

English word	Masculine meaning	Feminine meaning
This	este	esta
That	ese	esa
That (over there)	aquel	aquella (pronounced – aakeyaa)
These	estos	estas
Those	esos	esas
Those (over there)	aquellos	aquellas
This (neuter or no gender)	esto	
That (neuter or no gender)	eso	
That (over there-neuter)	aquello	

Este coche.	This car.
Esa iglesia.	That church.
Aquellos niños.	Those children (over there).

Esto, eso, aquello are used with the pronoun which are neuter or whose gender is not established. There are no plural forms of these words.

¿Qué es esto?	What is this? (Qué=what, es=is)
Eso no es correcto.	That is not correct.
¿Quién es Vd.?	Who are you?
¿Cuál es su nombre?	What is your name?
¿De quién es esta pluma?	Whose is this pen?

No es este libro, es aquél. It is not this book it is that one over there.
Estos zapatos son caros, ésos son baratos. These shoes are expensive, those are cheap. (son=are)

Exercise: -Translate them into Spanish.
This church, that church, this car, that car, these churches, those churches, these cars, those cars, this book, that book, these books, those books, this house, that house, these houses, those houses

New words: qué-what, es-is, correcto-correct, son-are, caros-expensive, baratos-cheap, su-your

¿Quién es Vd.?	Who are you? (formal)
¿Quién eres tú?	Who are you? (informal)

Lesson 13

Preposition

encima de	(entheema)	above
debajo de	(debaakho)	under
delante de		in front of
detrás de		behind
dentro de		inside
fuera de	(fweraa)	out of
enfrente de		against
cerca de	(therkaa)	at, near
lejos de	(lekhos)	away from
junto a	(khoonto)	ahead of
de / desde		of, from
sin		without
a		to
así		so
con		with

Un perro debajo de la cama – A dog under the bed.
Un libro encima de la mesa – A book above the table.
Unos hombres delante de la puerta – Some men in front of the door.
El jardín detrás de la casa – The garden behind the house.
Un gato dentro del coche – A cat inside the car.

Usage of 'de' – of
de + el = del; de + la = no change
El padre de María – The father of Maria.
Un fila larga de coche – A long line of cars.
Los dias de la semana – The days of the week.
Los dias del verana – The days of the summer.
Los meses del año – The months of the year.

The new words: la sortija – ring, la puerta – door, el gato – cat, el profesor – teacher, la escuela – the school, la cocina – kitchen, la estacion – season, el bolsillo – pocket, el pero – dog, el reloj – clock, oro – gold.

Exercise: -
A car ahead of the school. A ring inside the kitchen. The bottle above the table. The boy away from the church. The book of a teacher.

Make sure that you pronounce 'll' as 'y'.

Lesson 14

Los días de la semana

lunes	(loones)	Monday
martes	(martes)	Tuesday
miércoles	(myerkoles)	Wednesday
jueves	(khwebes)	Thursday
viermes	(vyernes)	Friday
sábado	(saabaado)	Saturday
domingo	(domingo)	Sunday

Los meses del año

enero	(enero)	Jan
febrero	(febrero)	Feb
marzo	(maartho)	March
abril	(aabril)	April
mayo	(maayo)	May
junio	(khoonyo)	June
julio	(khoolyo)	July
agosto	(aagosto)	August
septiembre	(septyembre)	September
octubre	(octoobre)	October
noviembre	(novyembre)	November
diciembre	(deethyembre)	December

Las estaciones del año

la primavera	Spring
el verano	Summer
el otoño	Autumn
el invierno	Winter

Lesson 15

Los Numeros

uno, una		one
dos		two
tres		three
cuatro	(kuaatro)	four
cinco	(theenko)	five
seis	(se-yees)	six
siete	(syete)	seven
ocho		eight
nueve	(nu-eve)	nine
diez	(dyeth)	ten

once	(onthe)	eleven
doce	(dothe)	twelve
trece		thirteen
catorce	(kaatorthe)	fourteen
quince	(keenthe)	fifteen
dieciséis	(dyethi-seyees)	sixteen
diecisiete	(dyethi-syete)	seventeen
dieciocho	(dyethi-ocho)	eighteen
diecinueve	(dyethi-nueve)	nineteen
veinte	(ve-eente)	twenty

veintiuno	twenty-one	primero	first
veintidós	twenty-two	Segundo	second
treinta	thirty	tercero	third
treinta y uno	thirty-one	cuarto	fourth
cuarenta	forty	quinto	fifth
cuarenta y uno	forty-one	sexton	sixth
cincuenta	fifty	séptimo	seventh
sesenta	sixty	octavo	eighth
setenta	seventy	novena	ninth
ochenta	eighty	décimo	tenth
noventa	ninty		
cien	hundred		
mil	thousand		
millón	million		

Exercise: -

Two men in the house. Three books in the car. Five days of the week. One child without the cloth. Four hotels near the garden. Nine horses near the sea. Ten boys one prize.

Lesson 16

la familia - family

los padres	parents
los parientes	relatives
el marido	husband
la mujer / la esposa	wife
el padre	father
la madre	mother
el muchacho / el chico	boy
la muchacha, la chica	girl
el hijo	son
la hija	daughter
el hermano	brother
la hermana	sister
le niño / la niña	child
el abuelo	grandfather
el tío	uncle
el sobrino	nephew
el prima	cousin
el suegro	father-in-law
el yerno	son-in-law
la nuera	daughter-in-law
el novio	boyfriend, fiancé
el soltero	bachelor
el parentesco	relationship
el matrimonio	marriage

Lesson 17

el cuerpo - body

la cabeza	head
el párpado	eyelid
la ceja	eyebrow
la cara / el rostro	face
la nariz	nose
el pelo	hair
la mejilla	cheek
el bigote	moustache
la barba	beard
la frente	forehead
el pecho	chest
el seno	breast
el pulmón	lung
el corazón	heart
el estómago	stomach
el hombro	shoulder
el brazo	arm
la mano	hand
el codo	elbow
el dedo	finger
la espalda	back
la pierna	leg
la rodilla	knee
el pie	foot
el talon	heel
la boca	mouth

Lesson 18

la comida – food

la comida	food, meal
el desayuno	breakfast
el almuerzo	lunch
el almuerzo	lunch
la carta / el menú	menu
la sal	salt
el restaurante	restaurant
la galleta	biscuit
el té	tea
el café	coffee
el agua	water
la bebida	drink
la leche	milk
el azúcar	sugar
la gaseosa	lemonade
la cuenta	bill
la bandeja	tray
la ensalada	salad
el cuchillo	knife
la cuchara	spoon
el camarero	waiter
por favor	please
gracias	thank you
el pan	bread
la mantequilla	butter
la naranja	orange
la uva	grape
la cena	dinner
el mango	mango

Lesson 19

el traba – work

el obrero	worker
el jefe	boss, chief
el gerente	manager
el empleador	employer
el artesano	craftsman
aplicado	hard-working / effortful
el taller	workshop
el comerciante	dealer
los parados	the unemployed
la oficina / el despacho	office
el rey / la reina	king, queen
el ladrón	thief
el dueño	owner
el vendedor	salesman
el dinero	money
el capataz	foreman
el músico	musician
el campesino	peasant / rural
el granjero	farmer
el soldado	soldier
el marinero	sailor
la licenciatura	degree
la escuela	school
el estudiante	student
el ejercicio	exercise
la lección	lesson

Lesson 20

la casa

la propiedad	property
el vecino	neighbor
el piso	floor
la dirección	address
el cuarto	room
la llave	key
el timbre	door bell
el jardín	garden
la madera	wood
la arena	sand
el pasillo	corridor
la escalera	stairs
la alcaba	bedroom
la cama	bed
la manta	blanket
el espejo	mirror
el cajón	drawer
el horno	oven
el forgón	stove
la fuente	dish
los muebles	furniture
la silla	chair
la mesa	table
la pared	wall
el tejado	roof
la ventana	window

Lesson 21

los animals y las aves – the animals and the birds

el nido	nest
la pluma	feather
la jaula	cage
la gallina	hen
el gusano	worm
el insect	insect
la cola	tail
la piel	skin
el pollito	chicken
el pato	duck
el ganso	goose
la paloma	dove
el cisne	swan
el gorrión	sparrow
el ruiseñor	nightingale
la corneja	crow
el papagayo	parrot
la mosca	fly
la hormiga	ant
la abeja	bee
la mariposa	butterfly
la araña	spider
el pez	fish
el perro	dog
el caballo	horse
la vaca	cow

Lesson 22

la ropa – clothing

el sombrero	hat
la corbata	tie
el vestido	dress
la falda	skirt
los tejanos	jeans
los pantalones	trousers
la chaqueta	jacket
el abrigo	coat
el sostén	bra
los calcetines	socks
el bolsillo	pocket
la zapatilla	slipper
el cuello	collar
el cinturón	belt
la bufanda	scarf
el pañuelo	hanky
la sortija	ring
la lana	wool
el algodón	cotton
la seda	silk
la tijeras	scissors
el género	cloth material
los pendientes	earrings
el collar	necklace
el guante	glove
la bota	boot

Exercise: -

The jeans with belt. A woman with the scarf. A cage without the parrot. The bed without blanket. This skirt is white. That slipper is red. This floor is clean. The tea with biscuit. July and September of this year.

Lesson 23

la ciudad – town, city

el pueblo	small town
el peatón	pedestrian
el transeunte	passer-by
el policía	policeman
el coche / auto	car
la bicicleta	bicycle
la motocicleta	motorcycle
la muchedumbre	crowd
la esquina	corner
los alrededores	surroundings
el aseo	toilet
la estación	station
el edificio	building
la iglesia	church
la biblioteca	library
el cine	cinema
el buzón	post box
el banco	bank
la comisaría	police station
la tienda	shop
el mercado	market
el museo	museum
la fábrica	factory
los semáforos	traffic lights
la calle	street
el parque	park

Lesson 24

el tiempo y el mundo – weather and world

claro	bright
la oscuridad	darkness
la helada	ice
el trueno	thunder
la bruma	mist
el relámpago	lightning
la tormenta	storm
la sombra	shade
la lluvia	rain
la nieve	snow
la luna	moon
la estrella	star
el cielo	sky
el país	country
la tierra	land, earth
el aire	air
el viento	wind
la flor	flower
el árbol	tree
la hierba	grass
España	Spain
español	Spanish
británico	British
Inglaterra	England
los Estados Unidos	United States
Alemania	Germany
Grecia	Greece

Exercise: -
The darkness with thunder. The rain without snow. This flower is white. That tree is old. The language of Germany. The weather of United States. Two men in the library. The ship of Spain.

Lesson 25

las vacaciones y los viajes – holiday and travel

el viajero	traveler
el turista	tourist
la habitación	hotel room
el ascensor	lift
la recepcionista	receptionist
la propina	tip
el recorrido	tour
la gasolina	petrol
el ferrocarril	railway
el andén	platform
el tren	train
la portezuela	door
el departamento	compartment
el aeropuerto	airport
el avión	plane
el horario	timetable
el retraso	delay
la aduana	customs
el barco	boat
el buque	ship
maredo	sea-sick
el piloto	pilot
el pasaporte	passport
la autopista	motorway
Bienvenido	welcome
Adiós	goodbye

Lesson 26

los communicaciones – communication

el libro	book
la carta / la letra	letter
el sello	stamp
el papel	paper
la página	page
la palabra	word
la frase	sentence
la pieza	play
el teatro	theatre
la música	music
el baile	dance
la canción	song
la prensa	the press
el periódico	newspaper
la revista	magazine
las noticias	news
la novela	novel
los anuncios	advertisements
el cuadro	painting
el sobre	envelope
el recibo	receipt
la receta	recipe
el mensaje	message
la carpeta	folder
el cuaderno	notebook
la taquilla	ticket office

Exercise: -

A notebook and a magazine. The tourist near the airport. The delay in the message. The land of Greece. The ice in the sea. The scissor is long. That bedroom is clean. My coat is white. March and April of this year. Saturday and Sunday of this week. This family is rich. The sparrow in the nest. Three and five is eight. The father of Maria is a teacher. The food of this hotel is expensive.

Lesson 27

verbos útiles – useful verbs

cantar	to sing
alcanzar	to reach
creer	to believe
coger	to catch
golpear	to strike
romper	to break
abrir	to open
cerrar	to close
tener	to have
saber	to know
hacer	to do
tomar	to take
tirar	to pull
traer	to bring
poner	to put
trabajar	to work
venir	to come
andar	to walk
correr	to run
saltar	to jump
leer	to read
escribir	to write
enseñar	to teach
aprender	to learn
olvidar	to forget
ver	to see
mirar	to look
llorar	to cry
oír	to hear
pensar	to think
avisar	to inform
reir	to laugh
explicar	to explain
llamar	to call
hablar	to speak
preguntar	to ask
acabar	to finish
ganar	to win

Lesson 28

palabras útiles – useful words

y	(ee)	and
o		or
si		if
en		in/on
sobre		on
entre		between
para		for
cada		each/every
pronto		quickly
tarde		late
con		with
sin		without
más		more
menos		less
aun		even
tanto		so much
mucho		much
algo		something
nada		nothing
nadie		no one
nunca		never
pero		but
también		also
porque		because
antes de		before
después de		after
luego		then
ahora		now
siempre		always
contra		against
hacia		towards
lejos de		far
muy		very
bastante		enough
demasiado		too much
así		so
todavía		still
casi		almost

Some more verbs: - ir = to go, dar = to give, jugar = to play, empezar = to start, amar = to love, entrar = to enter, comprar = to buy, pagar = to pay.

bueno	good
malo	bad
feliz	happy
triste	sad
raro	strange
peligroso	dangerous
inteligente	intelligent
tonto	silly
listo	clever/ready
estúpido	stupid
aplicado	studious
cortés	polite
grosero	rude
dulce	sweet
amargo	bitter
frío	cold
enfermo	ill
sano	healthy
salvo	safe
abierto	open
cerrado	closed
grato	pleasing
interesante	interesting
pesado	heavy
práctico	convenient
callado	silent
ruidoso	noisy
común	usual
fresco	fresh
profundo	deep
sabroso	delicious
loco	mad
inocente	innocent
culpable	guilty
preferido	favourite
distinto	different
enfadado	angry
útil	useful

Exercise: -

A notebook between the tables. This pen or that pen? The ship before the time. A little darkness and so much thunder. The boy is here but the girl is there. Less rain but more snow. A tour during holiday. The tourist already on the platform.

Lesson 29

modismos y frases – idioms and phrases

a causa de	because of
como de costumbre	as usual
a propósito	by the way
a veces	at times
lo mas pronto posible	as soon as possible
verdaderamente	really
rara vez	seldom
todavía no	not yet
ya no	no longer
si no	unless
al principio	at first
finalmente	finally
sin falta	without fail
por la mayor parte	mostly
ahora mismo	right now
por casualidad	by chance
por ejemplo	for example
todos los días	every day
en todo caso	in any case
una vez	once
una vez más	once more
otra vez	again
varias veces	several times
de buena gana	willingly
de mala gana	reluctantly
lo mismo que	the same as

Lesson 29 B
Unconjugative Pronoun

Yo	=	I
Tú	=	thou
Él	=	he
Ella	=	she
Usted / Ud. Vd.	=	you
Nosotros	=	we
Vosotros	=	thou people (ye)
Ellos	=	they
Eso / Él	=	it

*Unconjugative = Spanish drops pronoun and makes verb dependent sentences.

Lesson 30

expresiones - expressions

¿Qué hora es?	What time is it?
Son las tres.	Its three o'clock.
¿Qué es la fecha?	What's the date?
¿Cuántos años tiene usted?	How old are you?
Tengo treinta años.	I am thirty.
vale	OK
claro	of course
¡Qué raro!	How strange!
¡Cuidado!	Look out! / Attention!
¡Escuche!	Listen!
¿Cómo se llama usted?	What is your name?
me llama Pedro.	My name is Pedro.
buenos días	hello / good morning
¡hola!	hello
¿Qué tal?	How are you? / How things going?
¡Oiga!	Excuse me!
gracias	Thank you.
es verdad	Its true.
¿Cómos estás?	How are you?
¿Qué pasa?	What is happening?
a ver	Let's see.
¡Perdón!	I beg your pardon!
por favor	please
¡Siéntese!	Sit down
¿En qué puedo servirle?	Can I help you?
¿Cuánto es?	How much?

Lesson 30 B
Pronoun and Auxiliary

Yo + soy = (soy)	=	I am
Tú + eres = (eres)	=	Thou are
Él + es = (es)	=	He is
Ella + es = (es)	=	She is
Usted + es = (es)	=	You are
Nosotros + samos = (samos)	=	We are
Vosotros + sois = (sois)	=	Thou people are
Ellos + son = (son)	=	They are
Eso + es = (es)	=	It is

***Pronoun Collapse** = Spanish drops pronoun and makes verb based sentences to avoid redundancy.
***Force Pronoun** = Mostly non-natives apply pronoun by force to avoid ambiguity.
***Object Decline** = Some objects contracts (merge) with verbs.

Lesson 31

The Tense – Present Indefinite
Every Spanish verb ends in 'ar' 'er' 'ir'. Most of the tenses are formed by adding certain endings to the stem.

hablar – to speak

habl**o**	I speak.
habl**as**	Thou speak.
habl**a**	He/she/you/it speak.
habl**amos**	We speak.
habl**áis**	Thou people speak.
habl**an**	They/you people speak.

The stem of the verb takes **o, as, a, amos,áis,an** as an ending to form a sentence with regular verbs. The irregular verbs don't follow this rule. In simplified Spanish, pronouns are <u>used</u> to avoid ambiguity –
Yo hablo = I speak.

Affirmative

Hablo español.	I speak Spanish.
Hablan inglés.	They speak English.
Hablas ruso.	Thou speak Russian.
Habla alemán.	She speaks German.
Vd. habla griego.	You speak Greek.

Negative
While forming a negative sentence you have to place 'no' in the beginning.

No hablo ruso.	I do not speak Russian.
No habla Vd. griego.	You do not speak Greek.
No hablamos irlandés.	We do not speak Irish.
No habla suizo.	She does not speak Swiss.

Interrogative
To form an interrogative sentence only question mark comes at both end of the sentence. And the sentence is pronounced with interrogative tone. If Vd. or any subject is there, that comes after verb.

¿Hablan ingles?	Do they speak English?
¿Habla Vd. griego?	Do you speak Greek?
¿Habla suizo?	Does she speak Swiss?
¿Habla Sr. Martínezalemán?	Does Mr. Martinez speak German?
¿Habla el profesor españiol?	Does the teacher speak Spanish?
¿Hablan unos hombres?	Do some men speak?
¿Qué habla el guardia?	What does the policeman speak?
¿No hablo ruso?	Do I not speak Russian?
El niño habla.	The child speaks.

Translate into Spanish: - You speak Spanish. You do not speak Spanish. Do you speak Spanish? Do you not speak Spanish? What do you speak? The child speaks German. The child does not speak German. Does the child speak German? Does the child not speak German? What does the child speak?

Lesson 32
Other Verbs – irregular verbs

tener – to have (possess)

tengo	I have.
tienes	Thou have.
tiene	He/she/you/it have.
tenemos	We have.
tenéis	Thou people have.
tienen	They/you people have.

comer – to eat

como	I eat.
comes	Thou eat.
come	He/she/you/it eat.
comemos	We eat.
coméis	Thou people eat.
comen	They/you people eat.

vivir – to live

vivo	I live.
vives	Thou live.
vive	He/she/you/it live.
vivimos	We live.
vivís	Thou people live.
viven	They/you people live.

Examples –

Vivo en Londres.	I live in London.
¿Viven Vds. aquí?	Do you live here?
No hablo ruso.	I don't speak Russian.
No comen en el hotel.	They don't eat in the hotel.
Tenemos un libro.	We have a book.
Tienen una casa.	They have a house.
No tiene Vd. una pluma.	You don't have a pen.
¿Tiene Vd. una pluma?	Do you have a pen?
Pedro vive en Barcelona.	Pedro lives in Barcelona.
Come demasiado.	He eats too much.
El pueblo en el que vivimos.	The village in which we live. (en el que – in the which)
La casa que tiene una puerta verde.	The house which has a green door. (que tiene – which has)
La chica es alta.	The girl is tall.
Mañana es domingo.	Tomorrow is Sunday.
Tengo un sombrero nuevo.	I have a brand new hat.

Translate into Spanish: -

She does not speak Spanish. I do not eat in the hotel. They have a book. He has a house. You do not have a bag. She speaks too much. The boy is tall. Tomorrow is Tuesday.

Lesson 33
Verb 'ser' and 'estar' = to be

ser	estar	
soy	estoy	I am
eres	estás	Thou are
es	está	He/she/ you/it are
somos	estamos	We are
sois	estáis	Thou people are
son	están	They are/You people are

Ser expresses a permanent state.

Soy Lolita.	I am Lolita.
El reloj es de oro.	The watch is of gold.
Mi tía es de Londres.	My aunt is from London.
Son las cinco.	It is 5 o'clock.
Hoy es martes.	Today is Tuesday.
El padre de Maria es arquitecto.	The father of Maria is an architect.
Es difícil aprender.	It is difficult to learn. (es-it is)

Estar expresses a temporary state.

Alfonso está enfermo.	Alfonsa is ill.
Está en Mumbai.	He is in Mumbai.

Some words: -

qué (ke)	what		el que	the one
lo que	what, to what		de quién	of whom
que	who, which		cuyo	whose
quién	whom		cuál	what, who

Demonstrative Adjective: -

Masculine	Feminine	
este	esta	this
ese / eso	esa	that / it
aquel	aquella	that (over there)
estos	estas	these
esos	esas	those
aquellos	aquellas	those (over there)

When the gender of a thing can't be decided, then for this 'esto' and for that 'eso' or 'aquello' is used and there are no plural forms.

All Examples: -

¿Qué es esto?	What is this?
Eso no es correcto.	That is not correct.
Este cuarto.	This room.
Esta casa.	This house.
Aquellas sillas.	Those chairs. (over there)

¿Cuál es su nombre?	What is your name?
¿Quién es Vd.?	Who are you? (respect)
¿De quién es este libro?	Whose is this book?
¿Que habla Vd.?	What do you speak?
La chica que habla español.	The girl who speaks Spanish.
La ciudad en el que vivo.	The city in which I live.
El hombre que conoco.	The man whom I know.

Translate into Spanish: -
Who is he?
What is his name?
Whose is this book?
The woman whom I know.
What do they speak?
The boy who speaks Spanish.
The city in which we live.
They do not speak Spanish.
We have a car.
Today is Friday.

Translate into English: -
Pedro vive en Barcelona.
¿Tiene Vd. una pluma?
Tengo un sombrero nuevo.
¿Habla el profesor españiol?
¿Hablan unos hombres?
Vivo en Londres.
No comen en el hotel.

I can understand the difficulties you are going through while doing this exercise. As I mentioned before, the Grammar pattern of English and Spanish is different. Remember, if the task is difficult, the result would be great. Just keep moving.

Lesson 34
Possessive Adjective

Singular	Plural	
mi	mis	my
tu	tus	thy
su	sus	his/her/your/it
nuestro/nuestra	nuestros (-as)	our
vuestros (-a)	vuestros (-as)	of thou people
su	sus	their/of you people

Examples: -

Mi libro.	My book.
Mis plumas.	My pens.
Nuestra casa.	Our house.
Nuestros perros.	Our dogs.

The possessive adjective changes according to the thing, not according to the person who possess.
Sometimes, to avert the confusion of 'su' and 'sus' that means his/her/its/their/yours; we can use

Examples: -

de él	of him
de ella	of her
de Vd.	of you
de Vds.	of you people
El libro de Vd.	Your book.
El amigo de ellos.	The friend of them.

Possessive Pronoun

Singular (m/f)	Plural (m/f)	
mío, mía	míos, mías	mine
tuyo, tuya, tu	tuyos, tuyas	thy, yours
nuestro, nuestra	nuestors, nuestras	ours
vuestro (-a)	vuestros (-as)	of thou people
suyo, suya	suyos, suyas	of them, of yours

Examples: -

Este libro es mío.	This book is mine.
Este es mí libro.	This is my book.
La mujer con la que aquella el niño.	The lady with whom there is the child.
La señora cuyo libro aquel.	The Mrs. whose book is there.
No hablo lo que habla.	I don't speak what he speaks.
No come lo que como.	He does not eat what I eat.

Translate into Spanish: -
I don't eat what he eats.
The lady with whom there is the cat.
What do they speak?
The teacher who speaks English.
The city which is in America.
He has a brand new bicycle.
They don't live in England.
She doesn't speak too much.
The city in which we live.
They do not speak German.

Translate into English: -
Esta carpeta es mío.
La señora cuyo letra aquel.
¿Habla el niño palabras?
Vive en Barcelona.
Vivimos en Londres.
No comen en el hotel.
No comen lo que como.
La señora cuyo libro aquel.
Tengo un sombrero nuevo.

Lesson 35
Present Continuous Tense

This tense of regular verbs is formed by adding **–ando**to the stem of verbs which end in **ar**. And the verbs which end in **er** or **ir**, for that **–iendo**is added to the stem.

hablar – hablando = speaking
comer – comiendo = eating
vivir – viviendo = living

So, Present Continuous is formed using the verb forms of **'estar'**.

Estoy hablando.	I am speaking.
Estás hablando.	Thou are speaking.
Estamos hablando.	We are speaking.

Continuous Forms of regular verbs based on lesson 33: -

estoy hablando	estoy comiendo	estoy viviendo	(I)
estás hablando	estás comiendo	estás viviendo	(thou)
está hablando	está comiendo	está viviendo	(he/she/you/it)
estamos hablando	estamos comiendo	estamos viviendo	(we)
estáis hablando	estáis comiendo	estáis viviendo	(thou people)
están hablando	están comiendo	están viviendo	(they/you people)

Examples: -

Estás comiendo.	He is eating.
Vd. está viviendo.	You are living.
Estoy aprendiendo francés.	I am learning French.
Está bebiendo agua.	He is drinking water.
Este ascensor está lleno.	This lift is full.

Irregular verbs
There are some irregular verbs which don't follow any rule while changing their forms. <u>Even when they are used from Indefinite to Continuous Tense, their forms do not change</u>. I know it could be a little difficult to you but you have to bear with it.

ir = to go

voy	I go/I am going
vas	thou go/thou are going.
va	he/she/you go – going
vamos	we go/we are going
vais	thou people go – going
van	they/you people go – going

Relax; learning a foreign is a great job. Thanks to English for being so simple! Spanish is not like that. Please keep moving.

Example: -

Voy a Londres.	I go/am going to London. (a=to)
Van a la iglesia.	They go/are going to church.
Vamos a comisaría.	We are going to police station.

List of some irregular verbs: -
poner (to put): - pongo, pones, pone, ponemos, ponéis, ponen
dar(to give): - doy, das, da, damos, dais, dau
tracer (to bring): - traigo, traes, trae, traemos, traéis, traen
ver (to see): - veo, ves, ve, vemos, veis, ven
hacer (to do): - hago, haces, hace, hacemos, hacéis, hacen
saber (to know): - sé, sabes, sabe, sabemos, sabéis, saben
pensar (to think): - pienso, piensas, piensa, pensamos, pensáis, piensan
pedir (to ask): - pido, pides, pide, pedimos, pedís, piden
volver (to come back): - vuelvo, vuelves, vuelve, volvemos, volvéis, vuelven
salir (to go out): - salgo, sales, sale, salimos, salis, salen
ir (to go): - voy, vas, va, vamos, vais, van
venir (to come): - vengo, vienes, viene, venimos, venís, vienen

Translate into Spanish: -
(Use your ability – Google Translate will fail here)

I speak Spanish.
I am speaking Spanish.
He eats breads.
He is eating breads.
They live in England.
They are living in England.
I do not speak Spanish.
I am not speaking Spanish.
He does not eat breads.
He is not eating breads.
They do not live in England.
They are not living in England.
Do I speak Spanish?
Am I speaking Spanish?
Does he eat breads?
Is he eating breads?
Do they live in England?
Are they living in England?

Lesson 36
Present Perfect Tense
This tens is formed using present indicative of 'haber' = to have (not to possess). It is used just as a helping verb.

haber – to have
he	I have + (past participle)
has	Thou have + (past participle)
ha	He/she/you/it have + (past participle)
hemos	We have + (past participle)
habéis	Thou people have + (past participle)
han	They/you people have + (past participle)

Now, to form a past participle sentence of regular verbs, you have to add **–ado**to verbs ending in 'ar' and **–ido**to the verbs ending in 'er' and 'ir'.

hablar – hablado = spoken
comer – comido = eaten
vivir – vivido = lived
Some irregular verbs:-
escribir – escrito = written
ver – visto = seen
decir – dicho = told
hacer – hecho = done

Sentence Examples: -
He hablado.	I have spoken.
Has comido.	Thou have eaten.
Ha vivido.	He has lived.
Hemos escrito.	We have written.
Ha visto.	You have seen.
Han dicho.	They have said/told.

Objective Pronoun
me	me	te	thee
le/la	him/her/to it/to you	lo/la	to it (neuter)
nos	to us	os	thee (plural)
les	them/you	los/las	them (masculine/feminine things)

Challenging Examples: - (Object comes first in Spanish)
Lo he comprado.	I have bought this.
Una latra hemos escrito.	We have written a letter.
Han vivido dentro de Alemania.	They have lived in Germany.
El museo ha visto.	She has seen the museum.
Lo he dicho.	I have said it.
Mi hermana ha comido en el hotel.	My sister has eaten in the hotel.
El traba un obrero ha hecho.	A worker has done the work.

Lesson 37
Imperative and more... (serious lesson)

To make regular verbs imperative (order), you have to add **–e** to the stem of the verb ending in 'ar' and **–a**to the stem of the verbs ending in 'er' or 'ir'.

While making plural imperative, **–en**and **–an**is used. And Vd. is also added.

Hable Vd.	You speak.
Coma Vd.	You eat.
Hablen Vds.	You people speak.
Coman Vds.	You people eat.

Object is placed after the imperative unless it is negative.

Bébalo Vd.	Drink it.
Envíeselo Vd.	Send it to him. (lo=him)
No lo beba Vd.	Don't drink it.
No se lo envíe Vd.	Don't send it to him.

Some people use the object adding it with the verb at the end of a sentence:

Está esperandome.   He is waiting for me. (me = me)

The use of 'a' = to:

Llamo a Juan.	I call John.
Llamo a mi hijo.	I call my son.

No use of 'a':

Compra el libro.	He buys the book.
Tiene un perro.	He has a dog.

Living object first:

Me lo da.	He gives it to me.
Nos la lee.	He reads this to us.

When two 'le' come, first changes to 'se':

Se la envía.   He sends it to him.

The word 'a' used to avoid complication:

Se lo he dado a Vd.	I have given it to you.
La carta escribo a él.	I write the letter to him.
Los libros compro a ellas.	I buy books for them.

This lesson explains complex situation of Spanish. Spanish uses too many objective pronouns, and objective pronouns are polysemic.
lo = it, him, to him, to it, the, that
la = the, it, you – (all fem gender)
se = itself, oneself, all-self
le = to him, to her, to it, to you

Lesson 37 B
Survival Verb Forms

1. jugar = to play
yo juego, tú juegas, él/ella juega, nosotros jugamos, vosotros jugaís, ellos juegan
2. ir = to go
yo voy, tú vas, él/ella va, nosotros vamos, vosotros vais, ellos van
3. venir = to come
yo vengo, tu vienes, él/ella viene, nosotros venimos, vosotros venís, ellos vienen
4. comer = to eat
yo como, tú comes, él/ella come, nosotros comemos, vosotros coméis, ellos comen
5. beber = to drink
yo bebo, tú bebes, él/ella bebe, nosotros bebemos, vosotros bebéis, ellos beben
6. tomar = to take
Yo tomo, tú tomas, él/ella toma, nosotros tomamos, vosotros tomáis, ellos toman
7. dar = to give
yo doy, tu das, él/ella da, nosotros damos, vosotros dais, ellos dan
8. ver = to see
yo veo, tú ves, él/ella ve, nosotros vemos, vosotros veis as, ellos ven
9. amar = to love
yo amo, tú amas, éll/ella ama, nosotros amamos, vosotros amáis, ellos aman
10. pensar = to think
yo pienso, tú piensas, éll/ella piensa, nosotros pensamos, vosotros pensáis, ellos piensan
11. trabajar = to work,
yo trabajo, tú trabajas, éll/ella trabaja, nosotros trabajamos, vosotros trabajáis, ellos trabajan
12. comprar = to buy
yo compro, tú compras, éll/ella compra, nosotros compricomos, vosotros compráis, ellos compran

*In regular verbs, the stem takes:- o, as, a, amos, áis, an; but irregular verbs don't follow this rule.

Lesson 38
Past Indicative (onetimer)

This tense indicates that the work was done only once in past. And for this reason, this Past Indicative tense is same as Present Perfect tense. As already mentioned that **Present Perfect** is formed using 'haber' = to have (as a helping verb).

Sentence Examples: -

He hablado.	I spoke (one time) / I have spoken.
Has comido.	Thou ate (one time) / Thou have eaten.
Ha vivido.	He lived (one time) / He has lived.
Hemos escrito.	We wrote (one time) / We have written.
Ha visto.	You saw (one time) / You have seen.
Han dicho.	They said (one time) / They have said.

Lesson 39
Past Historic (multi-timer)

This tense indicates that the work was being done repeatedly in past. In Spanish, this tense is equal to 'USED TO' of English, like – 'I used to play', and also is similar to 'I was playing'. The verb forms for this tense change as per the following rule in both regular and irregular verbs. These verb forms must be used with <u>pronoun</u> to avoid ambiguity.

1. Verbs ending 'ar' takes: –
I – ba; thou – bas; he, she, you, it – ba; we – bamos; thou plural – bais; they, you plural – ban.
Verb – hablar = to speak

Yo hablaba	I used to speak / I was speaking.
Tú hablabas	thou used to speak / thou were speaking.
Él/ella/Vd hablaba	he, she, you, it used to speak / he, she, you, it were speaking.
Nosotros hablábamos	we used to speak / we were speaking.
Vosotros hablabais	thou people used to speak / thou people were speaking.
Ellos/Vds hablaban	they, you people used to speak / they, you people were speaking.

2. Verbs ending 'er takes: –
I – ía; thou – ías; he, she, you, it – ía; we – íamos; thou plural – íais; they, you plural – ían.
Verb – comer = to eat

comía	I used to eat / I was eating.
comías	thou used to eat / thou were eating.
comía	he, she, you, it used to eat / he, she, you, it were eating.
comíamos	we used to eat / we were eating.
comíais	thou people used to eat / thou people were eating.
comían	they, you people used to eat / they, you people were eating.

3. Verbs ending 'ir takes: –
I – ía; thou – ías; he, she, you, it – ía; we – íamos; thou plural – íais; they, you plural – ían.
Verb – vivir = to live

vivía	I used to live / I was living.
vivías	thou used to live / thou were living.
vivía	he, she, you, it used to live / he, she, you, it were living.
vivíamos	we used to live / we were living.
vivíais	thou people used to live / thou people were living.
vivían	they, you people used to live / they, you people were living.

Examples: -

El hombre vendía caramelos.	The man used to/was selling sweets.
Carlos compraba les libros.	Carlos used to/was buying books.
Ibamos a España.	We used to/were going to Spain. (ir = to go)
Vivía en la ciudad.	I used to/was living in a city.

Translate into Spanish: - I speak Spanish. I am speaking Spanish. I have spoken Spanish. I used to speak Spanish. I was speaking Spanish. I do not speak Spanish. I am not speaking Spanish. I have not spoken Spanish. I used not to speak Spanish. I was not speaking Spanish. Do I speak Spanish? Am I speaking Spanish? Have I spoken Spanish? Did I use to speak Spanish? Was I speaking Spanish?

Lesson 40
Past Perfect Tense
For this tense, you have to use past form of 'haber' as a helping verb like 'had' in English. In this tense, pronouns must be used to avoid ambiguity.

Yo había comido.   I had eaten.
Tú habías comido.   Thou had eaten.
Él/ella/Vd había comido.   He/she/you had eaten.
Nosotros habíamos comido.   We had eaten.
Vosotros habíais comido.   Thou people had eaten.
Ellos/Vds habían comido.   They/you people had eaten.

<u>Some negative words</u>
jamas, nunca   never   nada   nothing
tampoco   neither (not any of two)   nadie   no one (person)
ni -- ni   neither -- nor   siempre   always
algo   something   alguno   someone
también   also   o -- o   either -- or

Lesson 40 B
Comparative Adjective

bueno   good
malo   bad
mucho   much
poco   less
grande   big
pequeño   small
major   better
peor   worse
más   more
menos   lesser
mayor   bigger
menor   smaller

el más bueno   the best
el más grande   the biggest

Sentence examples: -
Un buen libro.   A good book.
Una buena pelicula.   A good movie.
El primer tren.   The first train.
Esta casa es más grande que la mía.   This house is bigger house than my house.
Este hombre es el más probe.   This man is the most poor.
Este edificio es más alto de Madrid.   This is the longest building in Madrid.
Esta novela es más interesante.   This novel is most interesting.

Lesson 41
Future Tense

hablar
hablar**é** (I will speak), hablar**ás**, hablar**á**, hablar**emos**, hablar**éis**, hablar**án**
comer
comer**é** (I will eat), comer**ás**, comer**á**, comer**emos**, comér**eis**, comer**án**
vivir
vivir**é** (I will live), vivir**ás**, vivir**á**, vivir**emos**, vivir**éis**, vivir**án**

Same rule with regular and irregular verbs.

Sentence examples: -

Vivirán con sus padres.	They will live with their parents.
Comerá con nosotros.	He will eat with us.
Hablaremos en Español.	We will speak (in) Spanish.
Vendrán con él.	They will come with him.
Diré unas pocas palabras.	I will say some (few) words.

Translate into Spanish: -
I eat.
I am eating.
I have eaten.
I used to eat.
I ate.
I was eating.
I had eaten.
I will eat.
She lives.
She is living.
She has lived.
She used to live.
She lived.
She was living.
She had lived.
She will live.
We speak.
We are speaking.
We have spoken.
We used to speak.
We spoke.
We were speaking.
We had spoken.
We will speak.

In Popular Spanish: -
'I will speak' = 'I am going to speak' = 'I go to speak' = Yo voy a hablar.

Lesson 42
Translation

He eats too much.
Come demasiado.
These children learn Spanish.
Estos niños aprenden Español.

He buys a newspaper.
Compra un periódico.
The village in which we live.
El pueblo en el que vivimos.

The woman who works in a shop.
La mujer que trabaja en la tienda.
What is the weather like?
¿Qué tiempo hace?

Today is very cold.
Hoy es mucho frío.
I don't know where it is.
No sé dondé está.

The book that I have to read.
El libro que tengo que leer.
It is Pedro who is a doctor.
Es Pedro quien es médico.

Whose letters are these?
¿De quién son estas cartas?
Which magazine is he buying?
¿Que revista está comprando?

The house which has a green door.
La casa que tiene una puerta verde.
The pen with which I write.
La pluma con la que escribo.

What is the number?
¿Cuál es el número?
Luis was smoking a cigarette.
Luis fumaba un cigarrillo.

'que' = infinitive 'to' / what / which / than

Lesson 43
Translation

He had worked in a factory.
Había trabajado en una fábrica.
The sea was very cold.
El mar estaba muy frío.

That church is very old.
Esa iglesia es muy vieja.
These friends are from Malaga.
Estos amigos son de Málaga.

This lift is full.
Este ascensor está lleno.
Those grapes are sour.
Esas uvas están agrias.

Those books are interesting.
Aquellos libros son interesantes.
It is that beach (over there).
Es aquella playa.

She is Italian.
Es italiana.
The apples are in the kitchen.
Las manzanas están en la cocina.

Madrid is the capital of Spain.
Madrid es la capital de España.
It is dangerous to smoke.
Es peligroso fumar.

They are on the beach.
Estan en la playa.
The weather is against us.
El tiempo está contra nosotros.

Maria prepares the meal.
María prepara la comida.
Carlos has not seen Toledo.
Carlos no ha visto Toledo.

Lesson 44
Conversation

Where is your father?
¿Dónde está tu padre?
He is in garden.
Está en el jardín.
And your mother, where is she?
Y tu madre ¿dónde está?
She is in the kitchen.
Está en la cocina.
Are you Mr. Davis?
¿Es Vd. el señor Davis?
Yes.
Sí.
I have a telegram for you.
Tengo un telegram para Vd.
Where is the telegram from?
¿ De dónde es el telegrama?
It is from London.
Es de Londres.
Oh! Thank you.
Ah! Muchas gracias.
Not at all.
De nada.
Hello! (Greeting)
¡dígame!(Both side exclamation mark)
Is that Alfonso?
¿Eres Alfonso?
Yes. Who is it?
Sí.¿Quien es?
It is Sylvester.
Soy Sylvester.
Hello! How are you? (Hello = informal greeting)
Hola! Comó estás?
Very well.
Muy bien.

Lesson 45
Paragraph

We are going to a village on the Mediterranean coast. The weather is very good. It is warm and the sea is lovely to bathe in. We like north better. Every year we go to Santander in August. But in north, it rains a lot and there are many days when it is impossible to go to beach. We are running away from the heat in Madrid which in August is unbearable.

Vamos a un pueblo de la costa de Mediterráneo. Hace muy buen tiempo. Hace calor y el mar está delicioso para bañarse. A nosotros nos gusta más el norte. Todos los años vamos a Santander en agosto. Pero en el norte, lluve mucho y hay mucho días en los que es imposible ir a la playa. Vamos huyendo del calor de Madrid que en agosto es insoportable.

Spanish uses many extra words in sentences – nosotros, nos.
To gain fluency in Spanish, refer to my next book 'Foreign Languages Conversation'.
You can also watch video conversation and movies.
Get some Spanish novels from the Internet to read.

To pass out Spanish A1 level, you need to appear for DELE A1 exam.
The best book for Spanish A1 is 'Aula Internacional A1'.

Lesson 46
Modal Verbs

poder = to be able to, can, may
Yo puedo jugar al cricket.
I can play cricket.
Ella puede cantar una canción.
She can sing a song.

podría = past of can
Nosotros podríamos compar un libro.
We could buy a book.
Ellos podrían ganar la carrera.
They could win the race.

deber = should, ought to
Él debería tomar café.
He should drink (take) coffee.
Tú deberías ahorrar dinero.
Thou should save money.

haría = would
Mark aprendería computer.
Mark would learn computer.
Justin comería mangos.
Justin would eat mangoes.

tengo que = have to
Yo tengo que hacer este trabajo.
I have to do this work.
Vd. tiene que venir aquí.
You have to come here.

tuve que = had to
Nosotras tuvimos que ir allí
We had to go there.
Ellas tenían que ser inteligentes.
They had to be smart.

After a modal verb, complete verb comes.

Lesson 47
Self-Introduction

My name is Niranjan Showman.
Mi nombre es Niranjan Showman.

I live in Mumbai, India.
Vivo en Mumbai, India.

My job is teaching languages.
Mi trabajo es enseñar idiomas.

I have written some books.
He escrito algunos libros.

I like to read books and watch movies.
Me gusta leer libros y ver películas.

My city is beautiful and rich.
Mi ciudad es hermosa y rica.

I have two brothers and no sister.
Tengo dos hermanos y ninguna hermana.

I am thirty-five years old.
Tengo treinta y cinco años.

I can speak English and French.
Puedo hablar inglés y francés.

My hobby is to visit new places.
Mi afición es visitar nuevos lugares.

Now I want to visit Europe.
Ahora quiero visitar Europa.

Speaking a foreign language is good for my career.
Hablar un idioma extranjero es bueno para mi carrera.

Europeans are great discoverers.
Las europeas son grandes descubridoras.

Thank you.
Gracias.

Lesson 48
My City Mumbai

Mumbai is a big city of India.
Mumbai es una gran ciudad de la India.

It is the financial capital of the country.
Es la capital financiera del país.

I live in this city from twenty years.
Vivo en esta ciudad desde hace veinte años.

Mumbai is thickly populated.
Mumbai está densamente poblada.

People have very busy life here.
La gente tiene una vida muy ocupada aquí.

Mumbai is famous for film production.
Mumbai es famosa por la producción de películas.

Many film stars live here.
Aquí viven muchas estrellas de cine.

Life is very expensive for all.
La vida es muy cara para todos.

There are many beautiful places here.
Hay muchos lugares hermosos aquí.

Local train is life-line of this city.
El tren local es la línea de vida de esta ciudad.

I like this for its beauty.
Me gusta esto por su belleza.

I live here for prosperity.
Vivo aquí por la prosperidad.

Mumbai is a cosmopolitan cit.
Mumbai es una ciudad cosmopolita.

I like this city for weather.
Me gusta esta ciudad por el clima.

Thank you.
Gracias.

Lesson 49
Our Country India

India is my country.
India es mi país.
I am an Indian citizen.
Soy ciudadana india.

Our country is in Asian continent.
Nuestro país está en el continente asiático.

Our national language is Hindi.
Nuestro idioma nacional es el hindi.

We have our national flag.
Tenemos nuestra bandera nacional.

Hockey is our national sport.
El hockey es nuestro deporte nacional.

Tiger is our national animal.
El tigre es nuestro animal nacional.

There are many rivers in India.
Hay muchos ríos en la India.

This is the seventh largest country of the world.
Este es el séptimo país más grande del mundo.

India is a secular democratic country.
India es un país democrático laico.

We have New Delhi as capital.
Tenemos a Nueva Delhi como capital.

We believe in peace and prosperity.
Nosotras creemos en la paz y la prosperidad.

India is an agricultural region.
India es una región agrícola.

It has many beautiful places to visit.
Tiene muchos lugares hermosos para visitar.

India has very nice weather.
India tiene un clima muy agradable.
I love my country.
Amo mi país.

Lesson 50
About Spain

Spain is a country in Europe.
España es un país de Europa.

Its neighbors are Portugal and France.
Sus vecinas son Portugal y Francia.

Madrid is the capital of Spain.
Madrid es la capital de España.

Madrid is also a beautiful city.
Madrid también es una ciudad preciosa.

Spanish is the national language of Spain.
El español es el idioma nacional de España.

Spain has fifty provinces.
España tiene cincuenta provincias.

It has forty-seven million population.
Tiene cuarenta y siete millones de habitantes.

Barcelona is the second largest city.
Barcelona es la segunda ciudad más grande.

This is famous for architecture.
Esto es famoso por la arquitectura.

Spain is famous for football.
España es famosa por el fútbol.

Festival San Fermin has global attraction.
Festival San Fermín tiene atracción global.

They play with tomatoes in La Tomatina.
Ellos juegan con tomates en La Tomatina.

Thank you.
Gracias.

Writing this book was really challenging to me.
I thank you for learning this much!
As you have reached here, now you need a <u>Spanish to English</u> dictionary.
Start reading the <u>SIMPLE</u> text of Spanish or refer to my next book "Foreign Languages Conversation".
If required, now you can do Spanish A1 certified course and ask us the detail.
Reading simple stories and watching videos will also be a great help.
Daily practice on what you have learnt is necessary to stop from falling down.
Expand your reach with confidence and enter the world of Spanish with gradual and continuous move.
Reading, writing, speaking and listening —do all the four things until you find yourself fully strengthened.
To do Spanish A1 course, you can contact us for further learning.
You have to pass DELE A1 examination for Spanish A1 level.

Niranjan Jha Showman
Trainer, Author, Physician, Entrepreneur, Filmmaker, Activist
Founder of Cromosys Corporation
facebook.com/cromosys
+91-9561450045
cromosys@yahoo.com
Nallasopara (W), Mumbai, India

Communicate with People

Listen to Them Carefully

Engage in Conversation

Develop Your Style

Read As Much As Possible

Speak Confidently

NIRANJAN JHA SHOWMAN

Founder - Niranjan Jha Showman

Education and Technology Research Center

Patankar Park, Nallasopara (W), Mumbai. +91-9561450045

Education, Technology, Publication, Healthcare, Newsmedia, Realtor, Filmmaking

www.facebook.com/cromosys

Cromosys Publication

Teach
Yourself
German

NIRANJAN JHA SHOWMAN

Cromosys Publication

Teach
Yourself
French

NIRANJAN JHA SHOWMAN

Cromosys Publication
Teach
Yourself
Spanish
NIRANJAN JHA SHOWMAN

Cromosys Publication

English Voice Accent and Pronunciation

NIRANJAN JHA SHOWMAN

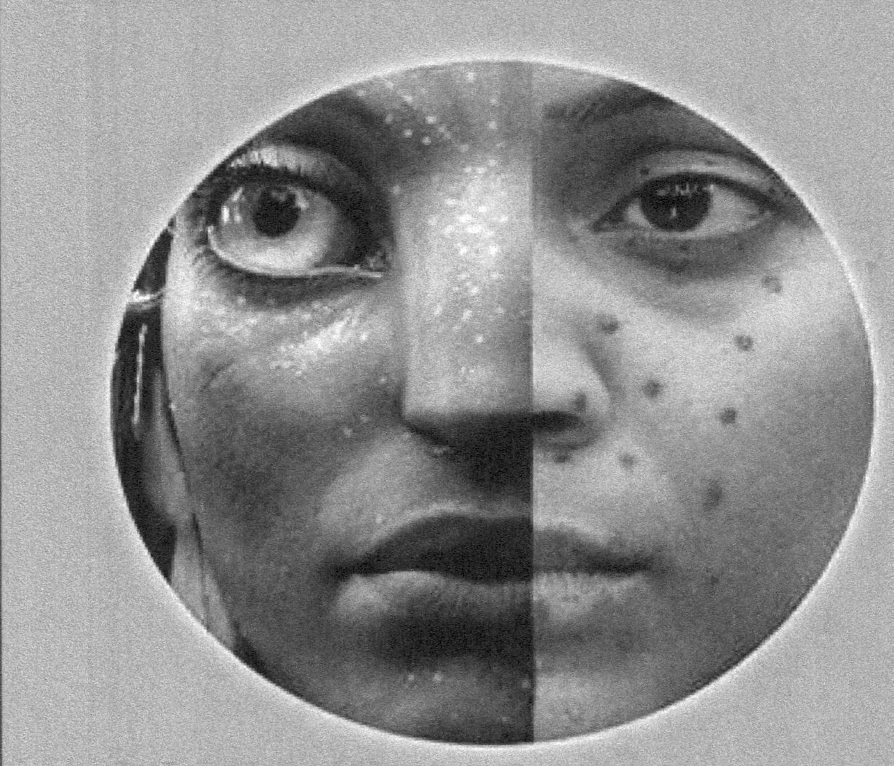

Teach
Yourself
Autodesk
MAYA
Cromosys Publication
NIRANJAN JHA SHOWMAN

Cromosys Publication
Teach
Yourself
Autodesk
3ds Max
NIRANJAN JHA SHOWMAN

Cromosys Publication
CRIMINAL FACTORY
NIRANJAN JHA SHOWMAN

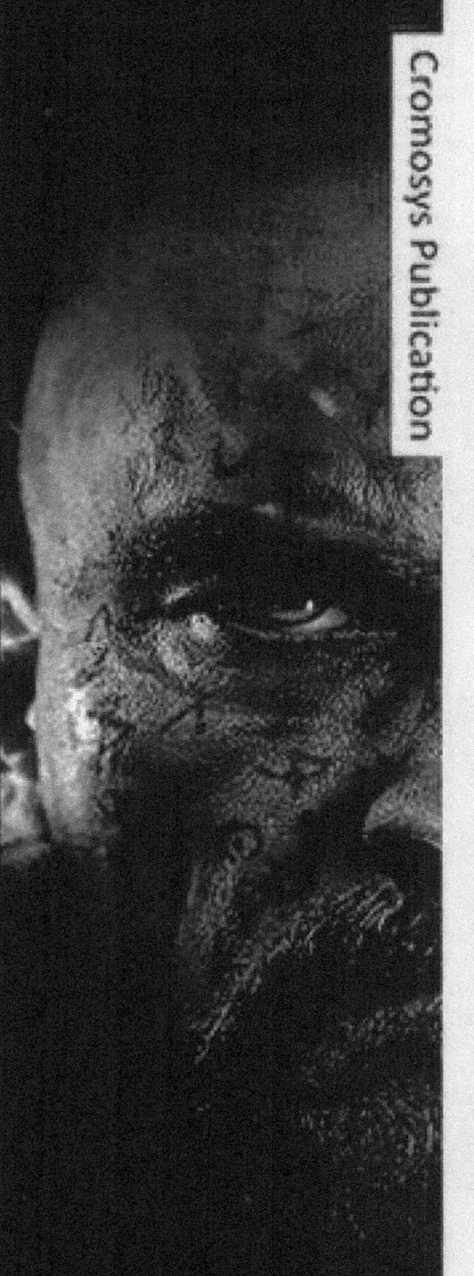

Cromosys Publication
FOCAL DISASTER
NIRANJAN JHA SHOWMAN

Cromosys Publication
Your talents will not help you succeed without your skill of using them.
NIRANJAN JHA SHOWMAN
BE
MILLIONAIRE
LIKE
ME

Copyright Office
Government of India

सत्यमेव जयते

Extracts
from the Register
of Copyrights

Dated : 22/07/2022

1.	Registration Number	:	**N-86768/2022**
2.	Name, address and nationality of the applicant	:	NIRANJAN JHA SHOWMAN, CROMOSYS PUBLICATION, 001, JAYSATYAM, PATANKAR ROAD, NALLASOPARA (W), MUMBAI, MAHARASHTRA - 401203. INDIAN
3.	Nature of the applicant's interest in the copyright of the work	:	AUTHOR
4.	Class and description of the work	:	LITERARY / BOOK
5.	Title of the work	:	**TEACH YOURSELF SPANISH**
6.	Language of the work	:	ENGLISH
7.	Name, address and nationality of the author and if the author is deceased, date of his decease	:	NIRANJAN JHA SHOWMAN, CROMOSYS PUBLICATION, 001, JAYSATYAM, PATANKAR ROAD, NALLASOPARA (W), MUMBAI, MAHARASHTRA - 401203. INDIAN
8.	Whether the work is published or unpublished	:	UNPUBLISHED
9.	Year and country of first publication and name, address and nationality of the publisher	:	N.A.
10.	Years and countries of subsequent publications, if any, and names, addresses and nationalities of the publishers	:	N.A. **SAME AS ABOVE**
11.	Names, addresses and nationalities of the owners of various rights comprising the copyright in the work and the extent of rights held by each, together with particulars of assignments and licences, if any	:	
12.	Names, addresses and nationalities of other persons, if any, authorised to assign or licence of rights comprising the copyright	:	N.A.
13.	If the work is an 'Artistic work', the location of the original work, including name, address and nationality of the person in possession of the work. (In the case of an architectural work, the year of completion of the work should also be shown).	:	N.A.
14.	If the work is an 'Artistic work', whether it is registered under the Designs Act 2000 if yes give details.	:	N.A.
15.	If the work is an 'Artistic work', capable of being registered as a design under the Designs Act 2000.whether it has been applied to an article though an industrial process and ,if yes ,the number of times it is reproduced.	:	N.A.
16.	Remarks, if any	:	

Diary Number :   5396/2020-CO/N
Date of Application : 05/05/2020
Date of Receipt :   05/05/2020

DEPUTY REGISTRAR OF COPYRIGHTS